D1402135

HIT THE DIRT

By Craig Robert Carey • Illustrated by Donna Reynolds

 A GOLDEN BOOK • NEW YORK

Golden Books Publishing Company, Inc., New York, New York 10106

Photographs: Cover, pages 2, 18, 19, 24, ©MSB®; pages 1, 16, 17, © Sandboard Magazine; pages 3, 6, 7, 21 (left), ©Nancie Battaglia; pages 4, 5, 8, 9, 11 (right), © Tony Donaldson; pages 10, 11 (left), 12, 13, 15, 20, 21 (right), 22, 23, ©Adventure Photo and Film; page 14, © Tyler Stableford.

EXTREME SPORTS

GET READY FOR ACTION!

Are you a really **"down to earth"** kind of kid? Then these extreme sports may be for you! Check out the mountainboarders rocketing down huge slopes, the extreme climbers scaling up whatever is in front of them, and the adventure racers competing in all sorts of demanding sports. Just turn the page to see some of these *amazing* athletes in ACTION!

MOUNTAIN BIKING

Don't let the name fool you: mountain biking doesn't just take place in the mountains. **Extreme** athletes ride through the **wilderness**, urban terrain, and deserts, too! They'll ride anywhere that's **OFF-ROAD**. Not even the snow stops them!

The thin tires of regular ten-speed bicycles weren't made to handle **rugged** conditions like these. That's why mountain bikes have much thicker tires and stronger parts. EXTRA gears were added to make it easier to ride up **steep** hills, too. In fact, mountain bikes can have up to 27 speeds for CRAZY climbing. Right on!

In 1994, **Christian Taillefer** broke the world speed record at a ski slope in Vars, France. He was clocked at 111 miles per hour! The mountain was so steep, people couldn't even stand on the slope!

Mountain biking **competitions** started in the 1980s. Popular events include cross country and uphill races. But one of the most extreme events is the Mammoth Mountain Kamikaze in California. It's a **WICKED** race that runs down the side of a huge mountain in the Sierra Nevadas. They don't call it **"kamikaze"** for nothing!

Another totally extreme biking competition is called **"the trials."** It's an obstacle course for mountain bikes, and it's wild. Some of the *obstacles* include boulders, logs, rivers—even park benches and parked cars. COOL! And bikers can't go around these obstacles—they have to go over them. Their feet can't even touch the ground!

STREET LUGE

Street lugers hop on a type of small sled with wheels. Then, they **BLAST** down mountain roads at more than 70 miles per hour—**feet first** and flat on their backs!

This sport is not your ordinary neighborhood activity. These sleds don't even have brakes! To stop, **lugers** have to drag their feet. To steer, they lean their body, tilting the board in the direction they want to go.

Do bacon and banana sound like a bad combination to you? They sure do to street lugers! In this sport, bacon is a road that's unsafe for luging. And a banana is someone who crashes really hard. OUCH! That's why street lugers wear helmets and thick leather suits. The gear protects them from injuries if they wipe out.

WE HAVEN'T EVEN STARTED YET AND YOU'RE ALREADY A BANANA!

Luge wheels move so fast on the road, they can melt, or even catch fire! Street lugers call this "spewing" or "flaming." Going superfast is called "wailing." Lugers sure WAIL!

ROCK CLIMBING

SHOW-OFF!

Hang on tight! Rock climbing is making its way to the top of extreme sports. Instead of carrying heavy gear, rock climbers barely carry anything at all! One reason they **pack light** is because, unlike mountain climbers, they're not climbing to get somewhere special. They're just climbing because a rock or a wall is there!

Even people in big cities are getting into rock climbing. Artificial **rock walls** are popping up all over the place, including school gymnasiums, so people can practice their skills.

Some of the basic equipment for rock climbing is really neat. For example, special clips called *carabiners* hold ropes to certain points on a rock wall. That way climbers fall only a little bit if they slip. The carabiners are hooked on to "BOLT HANGERS" which have been pounded into the rock.

EXTREME CLIMBING

Extreme climbers go places and make moves that once were **UNIMAGINABLE.** There's more than one way to extreme climb, too.

DUDE! I THOUGHT YOU BROUGHT THE ROPE!

Sport climbers use a rope, but it's just to catch them if they slip. Unlike rock climbers, they race against the clock or an opponent up a mountain or a rock wall.

Another type of extreme climbing is called **free soloing**. These climbers take a bag of chalk with them—but that's it, and they're climbing mountains! The chalk keeps their hands dry so they don't lose their grip.

BOULDERING AND BUILDERING

When athletes climb big boulders, they are **bouldering.** The climbs are pretty tough but not that far off the ground. So, if climbers slip or lose their grip, they don't fall very far. That's why almost all bouldering is done **without ropes.** People love it!

AWESOME! AND HE DOESN'T EVEN USE CHALK!

Guess what? Movie and cartoon characters aren't the only ones who climb up **skyscrapers!** Extreme athletes do it, too. It's a crazy style of free soloing called **buildering!** Like free soloing, these climbers just use chalk to help them climb. **WOW!**

SANDBOARDING

Watch out! Even without wheels, sandboarders are able to **"burn up"** hillsides with their **BLAZIN'** speed! On steep dunes, some boarders can go as fast as 40 miles per hour. Luckily, if they wipe out, the sand doesn't hurt much. But if **boarders** don't keep their mouth closed, they may be having sand for lunch. Yuck!

Sandboarding is an **excellent** sport for people who like to **travel** a lot. Because sand dunes aren't supercommon, athletes head for places like Saudi Arabia, Africa, Australia, and Mexico to do their thing!

The United States has cool places to sandboard, too. Some of these spots have dunes that are **hundreds** of feet high. Sandboarders can ride for over a quarter mile down these MONSTER DUNES! Far out!

HOT STUFF!

MOUNTAIN BOARDING

THIS IS BAAAAAAD!

In the 1970s, some **WACKY** skateboarders decided to put lawn mower wheels on their skateboards. When they started riding these **funky contraptions** down dirt hills and slopes, mountainboarding, or dirtboarding, was born!

Today, mountainboards are easier to **control**, especially on dirt. The tires still resemble lawn mower wheels, but they're specially made. Riders *steer* by leaning and tilting the board one way or the other, like in street luge.

International mountainboarding competitions are held all year long. The boarders in these competitions make some SERIOUS MOVES. With so many **hills** and **bumps** around, they catch air like you wouldn't believe!

DON'T WORRY ~ WE'LL CATCH UP IN THE NEXT EVENT!

Adventure racing may be the most extreme event, because it combines several sports in a **team competition!** It can include a 20-mile run through snowy mountains, then a mountain biking race through the desert, and then a difficult trek through the jungle. The athletes often have to be bused from one event to another. After all, it's not easy finding places that have all these **EXTREME TERRAINS!**

RACING

Adventure races have been held all over, including Argentina, Australia, Canada, New Zealand, and the United States. Superfreezing places aren't **out of bounds** either! The Iditasport and the Coldfoot Classic are two **popular** events, both held in Alaska. Extreme athletes race on bikes, snowshoes, skis, and run through the snow. BRRR!

Other adventure racing events include kayaking, canoeing, mountain climbing, and orienteering. In the orienteering event, RACERS don't even have a trail to follow—they're just given a map, a compass, and a se of instructions. Team members head for the **finish line** as fast as the can—wherever it turns out to be!

Many adventure races last several days. When athletes have to **compete** throughout the night, they often use headlamps. Some people call these "the TOUGHEST races on earth." And you know what? They just may be right!

SEE... TOLD YA!

WHERE TO LEARN MORE

There are all sorts of great places to learn more about your **favorite** extreme sports. Your local library and bookstore have books and magazines about many of them. And check out the Internet for some KILLER SITES, too!

HAVE FUN!

DATE DUE